Maestro Publishing Group

www.maestropublishinggroup.com

Hawking, Nate

How to Give a Hand Job: An Illustrated Guide. – 1st ed.

ISBN: 1451553528    EAN-13: 9781451553529

Book design by Maestro Eros.

Printed in the United States of America

# How to Give a Hand Job

## *An Illustrated Guide*

By Nate Hawking

# Contents

## Chapter 1: Introduction

The art of the handjob had gone neglected in the modern world. Well, maybe it hadn't been neglected in bedrooms but as far as books on the subject go, it really has. There are dozens of books on blowjobs, talking dirty, all kinds of sex but the art of the handjob had been tossed to the side.

Until now. Maybe this is the reason so many people are not very creative when it comes to satisfying their partner with their hands. Thus, the basic stroke or some variation thereof is what most people rely on.

Plus, handjobs are considered a sort of a precursor to sex and something that in itself does not contain much potential for fun or creativity. That's a mistake.

A handjob, when done properly and creatively, can be just as enjoyable and even more fun than a blowjob or just regular sex.

And when you've tried just about everything else, spicing up this part of your sex life can improve all the other aspects as well.

This book collects everything you'll need to learn the skills needed for an A class handjob. We will cover the Basic Stroke, Twisting Techniques, Double Hand Techniques, Tried and True Methods, even Prostate Play. In total, the book includes around 16 base techniques, all of them with illustrations and detailed instructions on how to apply them for maximum effect.

Tips for customization, combination of suggested techniques, even invention of your own will be covered throughout the chapters. The illustrations will make sure you're doing everything right.

We'll even cover the overall flow, from arousal to orgasm and how you should behave throughout the different phases of the handjob to achieve maximum effect. Turn the page and never let your handjob be boring or routine again.

## Chapter 2: Penis 101

Learning the basic anatomy of the penis is important so that you know how to please it better. Most of this might be obvious to many but for those that need a quick review, this chapter will do just that. So, let's study the physiology of the penis. Then, based on that, we can figure out how to simulate it in the most pleasing way.

Let's start with the basics.

The penis consists of two main areas, one being the head, which is also called the glans and the other one referred to as the shaft. These and other areas of the penis are illustrated in the drawing on the next page so glance there for an illustration. The glans is a very sensitive spot for most guys due to multiple nerve endings located there. At the same time, other areas also possess a high degree of sensitivity. One of those areas is the shaft. The shaft consists of three cylinders of sponge-like soft tissue. The shaft and the penis as a whole contain a high number of nerve endings and are sensitive to temperature, touch and pressure, even without any explicit thought of sex on the part of the penis's lucky owner. This is sometimes even true to the point of gaining an erection just by clothes rubbing up against it. When many men start playing with themselves as very young kids they don't make a connection with sex. It just feels good physically and that's what they do.

The other two important areas of the penis include the coronal ridge and frenulum. The coronal ridge is the rim that separates the glans from the body of the penis and the frenulum is a little triangle region on the underside of the penis which attaches a slender band of skin to the glans. The glans can be ticklish for many guys so keep that in mind. Again, the full physiology of the penis is illustrated on the next page.

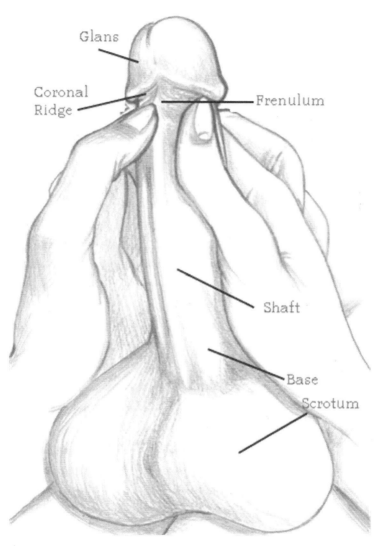

Figure 1: Penis 101

Despite the fact that traditionally the head is considered the most sensitive part, other areas have plenty of nerve endings too. A truly good handjob takes advantage of all or most areas shown above. That makes it more creative and fun. However, there are plenty of varying individual preferences. After all, there is a reason they say: "different strokes for different folks", pun intended.

When the penis is simulated through touch, the soft sponge-like tissue starts to fill with blood and the soft tissue becomes hard, creating an erection. There are of elements of precum generated as the penis is being simulated. Enough of that pleasurable simulation produces an ejaculation or release of sperm from the penis. After that, the penis gradually becomes flaccid again, unless, of course, more stimulation is applied.

Most men in the US have a circumcised penis. This is done either due to perceived medical advantages, religious beliefs or simply parental preference. And for those unaware, circumcised means that the foreskin on a penis has been clipped and pulled back to display the head while not being circumcised means that this foreskin stays in its place and is never surgically removed.

So, what's the difference between a circumcised and uncircumcised penis and why do we care about it?

There are some advantages to both versions. First of all, some people think that aesthetically a non-circumcised penis is more pleasing. Also, some medical studies showing hygienic advantages of circumcision gave the practice wider exposure, which has since then been disputed by some. At the same time, many women agree circumcised penis does not feel as good as a non-circumcised penis, due to the foreskin adding certain subtle but palpable stimulation. Here are some of the advantages to not having a circumcision.

1. Self lubrication during intercourse (due to the foreskin adding an additional effect).

2. Sex feels better for the guy due to the fact that some areas of the penis remain more sensitive due to being covered by the foreskin most of the time

3. Self lubrication during masturbation, which you can imagine is great for handjobs. So lube is not nearly as important for many uncircumcised guys.

4. Sensitivity does not decrease with age, unlike a circumcised penis that loses sensitivity through the head of the penis as it is being touched by clothes nearly all the time.

The foreskin itself is actually pretty sensitive itself so having it cut is already a decrease in the area for stimulation. There are nerve ending located all over the foreskin called stretch receptors and each of them can fire off when the foreskin is stretched, massaged or rolled.

The size and the shape of the penis are another consideration. While it seems like many men and women are obsessed with penis size, for the purpose of a handjob, the general logic and techniques will remain the same. Certain techniques may work better for a normal to large sized penis than for a smaller one but in general the logic will be the same, regardless of penis size.

And then there is the width or the thickness of one's penis. Width is important since having a thicker penis often makes stimulation more pleasurable and eases the application of some techniques. Usually though, a man has a penis that is on the longer side or on the thicker side, not both. Thus, the techniques to come should be adjusted for your partner's individual physiology and preferences. But, having said that a handjob is just as enjoyable for a slightly undersize penis as it is for a bigger one.

Now, this does not mean that men will stop competing against each other or that some women will not vie for the biggest man, but the fact remains true. Penis size is not a major factor when it comes to handjobs feeling better or worse.

Throughout this book we'll cover the technique needed for a great handjob as well as give you the tools to customize them and even come up with new ones. Whether you're inexperienced with sex or just want a little more creative advice, I'll try to make sure I have something for everyone to learn

The most important thing to keep in mind when it comes to a handjob is to reflect on what your man likes, his physical penis characteristics and of course, his personal preferences.

## Chapter 3: Prep Work

Now that we've got the basics down, let's learn about what it is we should do to set the mood. While stereotypes say that guys want immediate sex with no strings attached, the truth is foreplay is important and makes things more fun for everyone, especially in a long term relationship. Like most things, sex and orgasm are much more enjoyable if you build on to it gradually instead of rushing to conclusion too fast.

When it comes to foreplay, both people should be willing to do whatever it takes to satisfy the other person and make that the process is enjoyable to both, not just one of the participants. While handjob is usually not thought of as the main event during sex, a lot of the time a great handjob can serve as an intense part at the end of foreplay, something to do before you try a different pose during sex, or a way to get your man to ejaculate at any point. Also, if you're in a place where you can't easily have vaginal sex, handjobs often are used much more often.

Regardless of where in the actual intercourse the hand job will take place, setting the mood will be an important part of what takes place after. Some people like a more sensual experience, others like to get down and dirty. If you do want to add a little sensuality to it, follow Step 1. If you're not into that, skip on to Step 2.

## Step One - Light Some Candles, Add Some Music and Show Some Color

Foreplay isn't just touching and kissing, it can involve other things, from music to candle light.

Depending on the style of music that you two most enjoy could reflect very nice and sensual background music to your route of exploring his body with either your mouth or your hands.

I hear from some psychologists that different hues of colors can even promote moods or decline them, so when it comes to your coloring theme such as what your dress in (if your dress) or the color arrangement around the room, think about these color tips.

Red is for Passion
Yellow is for Cheerful
Blue is for Peaceful
Grey is for Gloom
Yellow, Orange and Red can be added together to create a warm mood. Therefore think of these colors when it comes to flowers, pedals or candles.


## Step Two - Get the Clothes Off

This could be anything from walking in front of him while stripping your clothes off until you are

11

standing before him completely naked and then stripping him down to nothing as well. Or you could take a different approach and work his clothes from his body using only your teeth. Another way to make it more fun is to be completely nude when he comes home from a day at work. This has a shock factor but it's definitely a positive, and most men would not object in the least if they'd find you like that waiting for them. Now, keep in mind, as you are teasing him or taking his or your clothes off, you can already give him a preview of what's to come. Here are the three main tricks you can perform when he has his clothes on.

**1. Bump and grind**. Whether you are dressed or not come up to him, turn away from him and rub your buttocks against his crotch. Try to curve your butt and really press it against him. Doesn't matter if he's hard or not, just do it. That feels really good for him.

**2. The Palm.** Take your palm, place it on his crotch and just massage it in, rubbing it around gently but firmly. Be sure to cover his penis as well as his balls. Once you reach the balls squeeze them lightly. This can be done as you are whispering to him or just kissing him.

**3. The Pinch.** You can grab the shaft of his penis and pinch it lightly. Then just squeeze it and look into his eyes. I am betting money you'll see that he likes it. Then squeeze it harder and harder and see what he thinks of that. He needs to be already hard or semi hard for this, otherwise it's just gonna hurt. Most guys like their penises squeezed pretty hard but be sure you don't hurt him so don't get carried away now.

## Step Three - Take it Slow or Fast, Depending on Preference

Hopefully, the techniques in this book will add more spice and fun to the handjobs you give him. However, as mentioned before, do not just rush into the handjob and be done with it. Remember through-out the whole process that your man wants just as much attention spent on them that you would want spent on you.

At the same time, if both of you are turned on by the idea of sudden sex out of nowhere, you can try the opposite.

## Step Four - Touch Him

Now we're done teasing his penis through his clothes and we actually want to proceed to direct contact. However, let's not rush. As you undress him, use your fingers, your hands, and your lips to play with his other areas. Neck, nipples, his belly button are always good areas to target. Touch, other than sight, is said to be the quickest way to give a man an erection and that doesn't even mean touching his penis directly. A kiss on the neck or a flick of your tongue against his nipple will often be enough to do the job.

Besides, doing this gradually builds anticipation and makes the game of sex so much more enjoyable.

Now what happens when you're actually down there and you're about to touch his penis?

Well, first of all, don't jump the gun. Take your time. I know very well that anticipation of sexual pleasure or simulation can be just as good as that sexual pleasure itself. So here are a few techniques you can use just before you dive in and start stroking him.

**1. Just Breathe**. That's right, just kneel if he is standing or crawl down to his penis when he is lying down and breathe on it. Don't touch it with your hands yet, just let your warm breath fall on his shaft, the breath on his head a little as well as on his balls. Be sure to look seductive as you do it.. He'll probably beg you to stroke him but don't give in, take your time.

**2. Touch Him Lightly.**

Tickling works very well to start. Gently tickle the shaft of his cock and his balls with your fingertips. Tease him a bit don't overdo it as it may become too frustrating for him. Then gently take his cock with your hand and squeeze it. You could do it with your fingertips over the head of his penis, you could go for the shaft or even the balls. Just make sure when you do grab him, you squeeze and rub and hold it nice and tight. Since otherwise he might feel like it's too much teasing and too little action.

**3. The Look.** As you are doing all of the above be sure to look at him seductively. Opening your mouth and licking your lips works great to. Often just the sight of his hard cock and your mouth wide open will be enough to fill him with lust.

Step Five- Don't Forget the Lube

First of all, the need for lubricant can depend on presence of the foreskin. If your man is uncircumcised, you can often just jerk the foreskin and that will feel great. However, without it, be sure to use plenty of lube.

Lubricants are indispensable for most handjobs. But how do you pick one? There are many different lubricants and each one has both advantages and disadvantages; here are some you can choose from.

**Water and Silicone Based Lubricants.**

These lubricants are some of the most common and are suitable for both sex and handjobs. Another consideration with lubes is if you intend to perform a blowjob, be sure you get an edible one (liking the taste of a particular lube will also be a factor)

Advantages of Water-based Lubricants

Wash off the body easily

More varieties such as flavored and warming on the market, easier to find

Not as expensive as most other lubricants

Advantages of Silicone-Based Lubricants

Do not absorb into the skin like water-based lubricants

Do not contain water which means it will never evaporate

Can be more expensive

**Organic Lubricants**. Organic means that the lubricant was made from purely grown ingredients and not from any sort of chemicals. So if you're worried about chemicals and unnatural stuff, go for these. Although in my experience, the artificial flavors taste better.

**Specialty Lubricants**. Flavored lubricants and warming lubricants can be an interesting addition to spice up a handjob. You may want to consider this after you've already tried it with a regular lube

**Oil Based Lubricants.** While all of the above have advantages and disadvantages, as far as handjobs are concerned, the very best lubricant you can use is an oil-based one. This is because of its ability to stay slick longer, thus being optimal for a handjob. At the same time, this type of lube is generally not recommended for intercourse or use with condoms. So, I'd say go with this type but people are different and you may find something works better for you and your man. So, explore since tastes vary. One suggestion would be to try many different types of lubricants with your partner before sticking to one. After all, having several different types around could add more flare to a sexual relationship by itself.

So, lube his penis up and get ready for fun. You can warm the lube on your hands before applying it to his penis so it feels warm for him. Or, instead you could pour the lube straight on his penis, if you think he'd like it.

We're done with set up, let's move on to technique.

## Chapter 4: The Basic Stroke

Just like kissing or sex, a handjob is (or should be) more than just monotonous, repetitive motion. Don't get me wrong, doing the same thing each time works once or twice, but there is a much better way of getting the job done if you know more than just one stimulation technique. So, remember, when you are giving your guy a handjob, it's more than just about moving your hand in an up and down motion.

Every man has 0.8 second intervals when it comes to their orgasm, which by the way is the same as a woman. The longer the period for which a man is stimulated before his orgasm, the more explosive the orgasm will be. So, whatever technique you decide to use, remember not to rush. Put these together in a sequence and patiently make your way to the grand finale. He will be very grateful.

### The Basic Stroke

So, how do you actually start? Before you use any technique, take his cock between both hands, with your left hand holding the shaft and your right hand cupping the head. Your left hand should slightly jerk in an up and down motion as your right hand begins to circle the head. This will both stimulate the head and the shaft, making sure that he is getting the maximum pleasure from this. Stimulating these two areas is part of the basic stroke. Note that depending on the size of the penis you're dealing with, the below may be more or less viable. You can stimulate just the top part of the shaft, just the bottom one, or both as shown in the drawing below.

Figure 2: The Basic Stroke

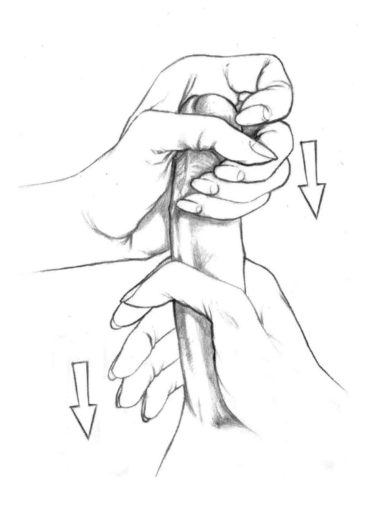

These are the two main areas of penis stimulation. Note that there are many other ones like the balls and so on but most techniques rely primarily on the head or the shaft stimulation, Now that we understand the methodology of the basic stroke, let's look at a few variations that will make the basic stroke a little more interesting.

**1. The Thigh Swatter.** As you are giving him a hand job, slowly start swatting his thigh with your other hand, which is a very sensitive area for many. You do not have to do it roughly, simple love taps will do.

**2. Switch Hitter.** This technique involves switching the holding of his penis between your left hand and your right. Alternating hands feels different and many men like. As you are switching, keep your up and down motion going and try not to let your motions become too weak.

**3. Bookends.** This technique involves placing both your hands on either side of his penis as though you were its bookends. You will then start to squeeze your hands together. Firmly glide them up and down as you're doing that.

**4. Milking.** Place one hand at the bottom of his penis and hold it there tightly. Slowly began stroking the penis from the bottom all the way to the top. Once you've reached the tip, let go. Use your other hand to repeat the same motion.

**5. Ring.** Use your thumb and forefinger to make a ring which you will use to pump up and down. As you get to the head of his penis you will make the ring tighter. Use this tightened hold to slide your hand back down toward the base.

**6. Spot Pinch.** With one finger, slowly glide it along the underside of his penis until you have reached the head. Once there begin to squeeze, pinch it in round motions.

**7. Fire.** Take both palms and hold his penis on either side and imagine you're making a fire. Just like you'd use sticks to run together, rub his penis between your hands. However, more oil is usually required to use this trick so keep this in mind.

**8. Pulsing Head.** Place your hands on the head of his penis, squeeze tightly and then let go. Then grab a hold of the head again. This can be done as he is ejaculating and can be timed with his contractions.

**9. Scarf or Gloves.** To try something different, try using a silk or chiffon scarf or gloves while you play with him. Wrap it around his penis however you would like and use your hands to grab him through the scarf. You can use gentle up and down motions and even twist occasionally. You can use your hands to give him the needed motions or you can let the scarf do all the work. Depending on the material and how it's used, the way it feels for your man will vary as well.

**10. Peaking.** If you want to try something different and want to tease your man a little bit this trick could come in quite handy.. As you feel he is getting close to coming pull your hand away and spend time doing anything else to his body, like rubbing his thigh. Then go back to the handjob and repeat until you feel he is about to come then let go again. This is fun as it will tease him and he will practically beg you to finish him off. And when it does come, it will feel a lot better for him due to all the accumulated tension. Just be sure not to overdo it as he could get a little overly frustrated. I wouldn't repeat more than 2-3 times in a row, unless he states that he likes it.

In summary, when you are giving your man a handjob the most important thing to think about is spontaneity and diversity. Use a different technique every time you give him a handjob but always incorporate his favorite one through-out every handjob he receives.

## Chapter 5: Twisting Techniques

Last chapter explored the basic stroke as well as its variations

In this chapter, we will talk about some twisting techniques that will add spice to your hand jobs. Twisting may sound like a very harsh thing to do to your guy's penis but, don't worry, when done the right way, it can leave your man begging for more.

So, without further ado, here are some twisting techniques you should consider integrating into your hand job routine.

**The Corkscrew.** Here is how we'll do this one. Use the thumb and index finger of your one hand to create a ring which you will place at the base of the penis. Use the thumb and index finger of your other hand to create a ring at the very top of the shaft. After this, twist the fingers of your both hands as you slide them along the base of the penis to meet together in the middle of the shaft. This technique is further illustrated in the drawing below.

Figure 3: The Corkscrew

**Swizzle Stick.** This technique is a lot like the Corkscrew. However, with this one you will wrap your whole right hand along the top of his shaft and your whole left hand around the base of it, instead of using just index finger and thumb. The twisting motion and hands meeting in the middle remains the same.

Figure 4: Swizzle Stick

**The Reverse Stretch.** This twisting technique applies pressure on the base of the penis and simulates the shaft, generating a very pleasurable sensation. To do this take one hand and press it against the base of the shaft, putting pressure on it. Use your other hand to stroke the penis up and down. Illustration is on the next page.

Figure 5: The Reverse Stretch

**The Palmster.** This one is a slight variation on the basic stroke. To perform this right, place the palm of your hand on the head of the penis and use circular motions to stimulate it. The other hand should be stroking the shaft up and down, as illustrated below.

Figure 6: The Palmster

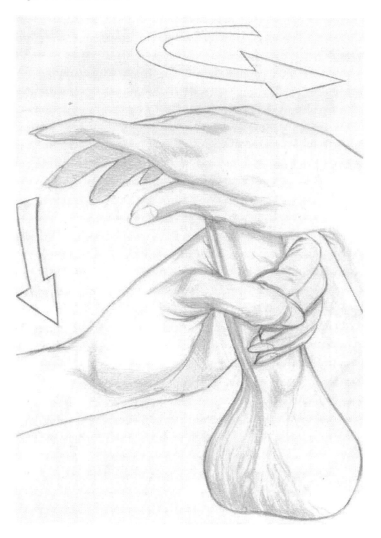

## The Grip

This one is good when your hands tired or just to switch things up. Just grip the base of his pennies and squeeze it nice and tight. Be sure to twist the base back and forth a little, and shake the rest of the penis as you do that. This one usually feels great but don't overdo the twisting as too much pressure may be painful.

Figure 7: The Grip

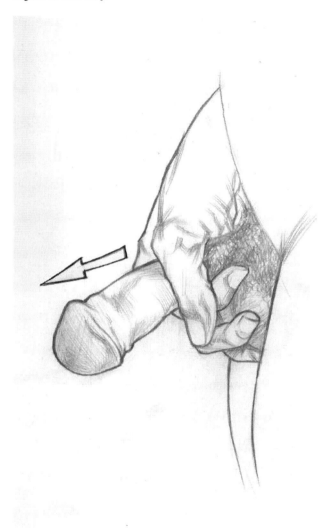

## Chapter 6: Double the Pleasure

When people think hand jobs they think about penis stimulation and that makes sense. However, his balls and perineum also need attention if you want to make the most out of your handjobs.

The perineum, also referred to as the "taint" is a small triangular area and is located between the testicles and the anus and can be a very sensitive area for both women and men. Adding sexual touches to this area while giving your man a handjob can make the sensations more pleasurable and help build up to a more powerful orgasm. His perineum often feels hard and although it might feel odd at first to stimulate it, there are a lot of nerve endings there, thus making its stimulation very pleasurable.

You can stimulate it at any point during a handjob, blowjob or even during intercourse. Sometimes it's good to stimulate it is right before he has an orgasm. Be sure to use your knuckle or your index finger for stimulation though to make sure you don't scratch them.

Thus, these techniques will make sure that you don't neglect other areas of your man's body that are almost as sensitive as the penis.

**Cup Runneth Over.** Stroke his shaft with one of your hands in an up and down fashion and squeeze his balls with your other hand. Be sure to not put too much pressure on the balls, find out what he likes and base it off that. This technique is further illustrated on the next page.

Figure 8. Cup Runneth Over

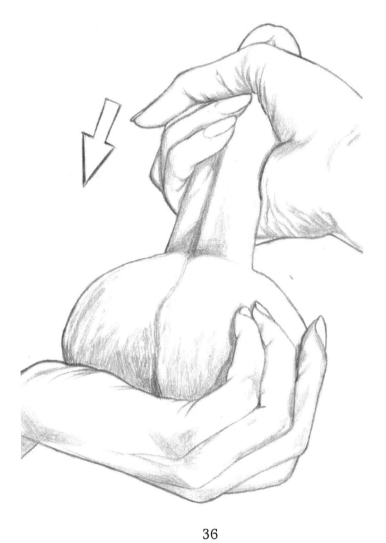

**Double Slide.** Start by stroking his shaft with one of your hands, then take the middle finger and index finger of your other hand and slide it along the his balls in a sexy circular motion over and over. The difference here is subtle but is a huge turn on for many guys. This is illustrated in an exhibit on the next page

Figure 9: Double Slide

**The Tickler.** Tickle his testicles with your left hand while your other hand strokes his penis. Experiment with teasing the tip of his penis by slowly twisting the head between two fingers. View the illustration on the next page.

Figure 10: The Tickler

Creativity is very important when it comes to sex and all of these techniques can be modified and combined to suit your and your partner's individual preferences and requirements.

## Chapter 7: Backdoor Fun

We've covered the balls and the penis, which are the primary areas people think about when they think about handjobs. What, you mean there is something else? Actually, there is! That's right, I am referring to anus and prostate play. Now many men and women are uncomfortable even thinking about the idea. Many believe it to be somehow unmanly or unappropriate. Morals are subjective and if this isn't your or your man's cup of tea, skip on ahead. But, all reservations aside, it does feel good and many guys do enjoy it. So this is a good reason to include it in this little book.

The prostate gland is a small ball the size of a walnut and is located behind the base of your man's penis right below the bladder. The prostate gland is often referred to as the man's g-spot or even more recently as the p-spot. In general, playing with the prostate can feel very good for a man.

Now, keep in mind that if you do intend to stimulate his prostate, you are putting hands inside his anus and a lot of things that could go wrong there. First of all, make sure that your hands are clean and that he had a nice soapy bath beforehand. Area of prostate play alone requires much more detail than this book can give it so research it on your own so you can practice it safely. Second of all, if you have long fingernails, prostate play is not a good idea. Thirdly, if you do decide to do it, perform it gradually, don't just stick a finger up his butt. Being gentle and taking your time is paramount as the skin there is very easy to rip, which you don't want as it's both scary and dangerous. I'd advise you to do some more outside research on anal play if you've never tried it before. Having said that, the main principles are below.

First and foremost, wash your hands.

Secondly, relax. Anal play can be very nerve-racking espeically if this is the first time that you have ever tried it. It doesn't matter if you are giving or receiving, it can still generate quite a bit of anxiety. So before you try it out with your man, take the time to do something that makes both of you relax.

As mentioned before, before you try this, trim down your nails and smooth out any rough edges. The lining of his anus is very tender and extremely sensitive which means it can tear easily and you will end up causing him more pain than pleasure. If you have long acrylic nails then you may want to think about using latex gloves to ensure his safety during this massage (or maybe not try it at all).

43

Make sure your man is completely relaxed and comfortable before beginning. Don't just start doing it without warning. Not every guy is comfortable with this and even if he is you both may need preparation. Prostate massage isn't something you normally do just at the spur of the moment.

Your first step once he is already aroused is to use lubrication. Once you have sucessfully lubed your hand up, you'll want to take things very slowly. Some men have experimented on their own when it comes to anal play while other men have no such experience and need things taken extra slowly. You can start at his perineum and use some of the techniques to simulate him there. After which, you can continue on to his anus which you can rub on the outside before letting your finger slide in. Just gently push at his sphincter so that it will help relax him and get him prepared for the intial entrance.

Once you're in be sure to just let it rest their for a few moments before trying something else. This should relieve some anxiety and let him get used to you being inside of him without too many things going on at the same time.

Make sure he breathes and is relaxed. Being relaxed and breatheing is the key to comfortable anal play. He should try and breathe in and out slowly while you are inserting your finger inside of him. Once you are inside his anus and you have given him some time to open up around your finger, than you should locate his prostate. If he is aroused, than this should not be a hard step at all. Within two inches inside his anus, you should be able to locate his prostate. It will be found in the direction of your man's belly so once you're in two inches look around for it and it should be somewhere on the upper side. Once you have found it, touch it lightly to let your man get a feel for what you are doing. Again, be sure not to rush and take your time with this process.

Once you have tried touching it a bit and your guy seems comfortable with it, you can use prostate play and combine it with stroking his cock to make it a lot more fun for him. The more often you do this, the easier it will get and after a while the process of relaxation won't be as long or as burdensome. View the illustration on next page to see exactly how prostate play can be combined with a handjob.

Figure 11: Prostate Play

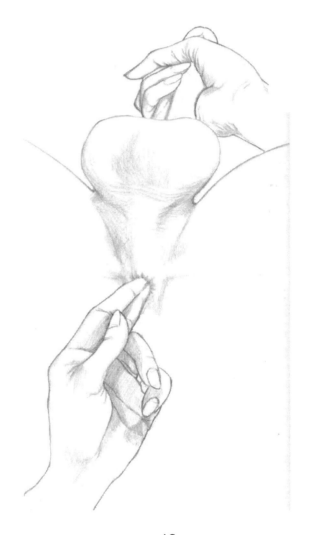

**Taint Love.** Try stroking his penis with one hand while pressing a few knuckels agains his pirenium (area between his balls and his anus). This is illustrated on the next page.

Figure 12: Taint Love

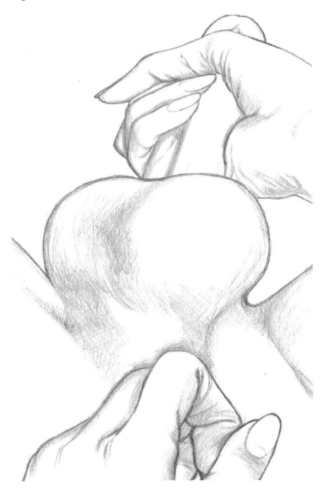

**The Three Way.** This techique stimulates the penis, the perineum and the anus at the same time, making it both extra pleasurable for the guy and a lot of work for you. Nevertheless, here is how you do it. One of your hands should be stroking the shaft of the penis, while the index finger of the other hand should be inside the anus as the thumb should be pressed against the perineum at the same time. The drawing on the next further illustrates this.

Figure 13: The Three Way

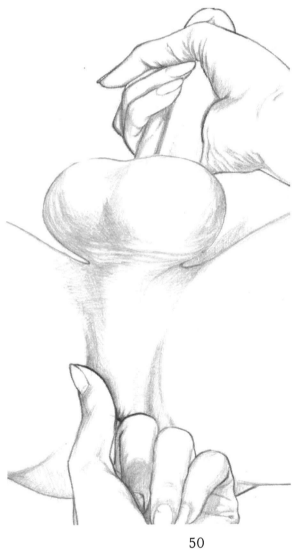

## Chapter 8: Tried and True

We've covered a few types of handjobs by now, starting with the basic stroke all the way to prostate play. Despite the fact that adventurousness and variety are important, sometimes keeping it simple is the best way to go. This chapter will explore some techniques which emphasize simplicity and focus on the penis as opposed to getting the surrounding areas involved.

So, without further ado, here they are.

**The Warm Up Stroke**. This one is simple but is very good to use in the beginning stages of the handjob, when his penis is still semi hard. To do this, just place one of your hands tightly around the base of his shaft and slowly glide it all the way up to the hand in a smooth sexy motion. Then repeat with the same or the other hand. The illustration on the next page provides further insight in how to do this.

Figure 14: The Warm Up Stroke

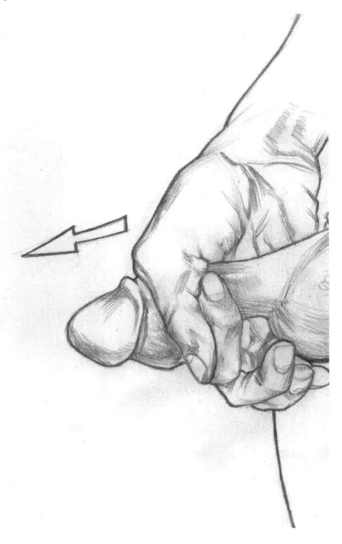

**Thumb Twiddler**. First of all, have your man lie back so that you can sit between his legs. Grab his penis with both hands and start to twiddle your thumbs together beneath the frenulum, which is the small flap on the underside of his head. This area is very sensitive so make sure you take it easy at first. This is illustrated on the next page.

Figure 15: Thumb Twiddler

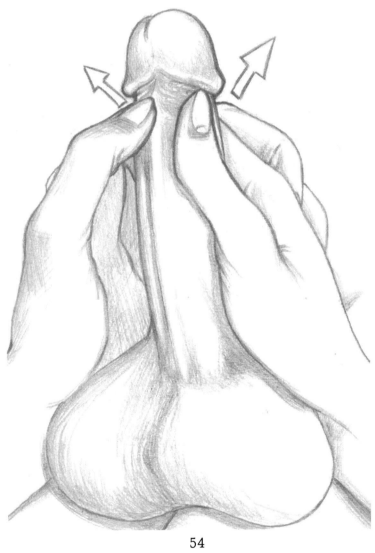

**The Anvil Stroke.** Grasp his penis with one hand at the top, slide it all the way down to the bottom and release it and then repeat the same with the other hand. Continue to alternate hands as you keep moving forward. View the illustration on the next page.

Figure 16: The Anvil Stroke

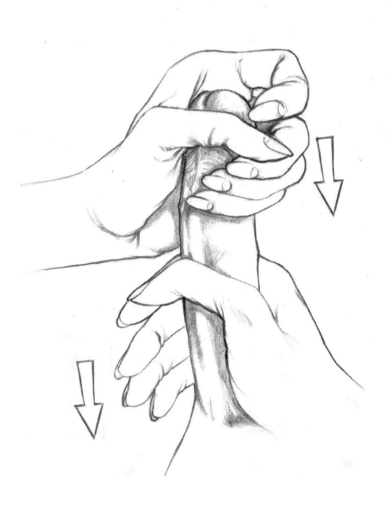

**Tango for Two.** Take both of your hands and slide them up and down the full length of the shaft. This covers the whole penis and provides non stop stimulation to your man.

Figure 17. Tango for Two

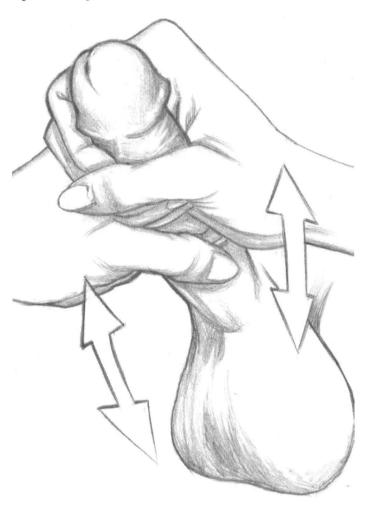

## Chapter 9: Customizing the Techniques

Obviously, the techniques outlined above are not set in stone. These were just some we were able to come up with. They can be further combined, reorganized or slightly rearranged to suit your particular needs.

So, how do you go about being creative and customizing these to fit your needs? A good place to start would be to watch your man masturbate, see how he does it and pick it up from there.

Most men have been giving themselves handjobs since they first hit puberty. So in general most men are pretty good pleasuring themselves in this way due just to the sheer experience they've had doing it. So before you start to get creative, have him show you exactly what he does like through demonstration. Just place your hand over his and let him do all the work until you feel confident to take over. Some women feel a bit insecure when it comes to their man showing them how it is done. Don't let this trouble you. You are asking him for advice in that department which shows you are interested in pleasing him, not that you are inexperienced. And it really isn't that complicated once you get the hang of it.

Now, if it was as simple as that, you really wouldn't need a whole book to help you through this.

<u>Starting Experimentation</u>

Be sure to follow the following principles when you start to apply the techniques in this book to the list of your bedroom activities:

1. Start with the basics.

The basic stroke as well as everything in the Tried and True section are all good techniques to start with.

2. One thing at a time.

There are quite a few techniques in the book. Try doing too many things at once and you can get overwhelmed or confused. Thus, for every time you anticipate giving your man a handjob, take 2-3 techniques and really make sure you remember them, then focus on playing with him just using those.

3. Master what you know before moving on.

Before you go on and expand to more complicated techniques, spend a few times applying the more basic ones and make sure you have got a good mastery of them. Doing all things at the same time often leads to doing none of those things very well. Thus, be sure to take your time before you move on.

4. Stay spontaneous.

It is very important that your handjob does not feel too planned or inflexible. Spontaneity is a big part of doing it well. Thus, it's fine to have an approximate plan of what techniques you'll use but adjust it to circumstances and be sure to try it differently each time as variety is good.

What happens when you've mastered and applied all of these techniques and you're ready to try something new and creative? Obviously, if the formula to creativity could be pinned down so easily, it wouldn't be creativity. Despite that, here are some principles to help you take the outlined techniques and make them into something new.

1. Principle of Combination

Very often taking two different techniques and combining them can produce an effect different enough to warrant alteration. For example, look at The Palmster technique. This one involves rubbing one hand around the penis's head and using the other hand to stroke the shaft. Now, imagine you wanted to combine this technique with another one. Let's pick Cup Runneth Over. This is a technique using which you stroke his shaft with one hand and squeeze his balls with the other. Obviously, there are many different ways to do this. But a good one would be to substitute ball squeezing for the stroking in the Palmster. Thus, you still will use one hand to rub the head of the penis (As Palmster tells you) but with your other hand you will now squeeze the balls as in Cup Runneth Over (instead of stroking the penis). As you can see, this can lead to an innumerable number of variations, where you could play with his taint as you are rubbing the head of his penis, pulling on his balls, rubbing his shaft in milking motion, dozens of other options.

Not all of these have to be thought out and preplanned. Once you have mastered all of the mentioned techniques you can combine them as you go along and let your creativity take rein. Eventually, you won't even think about them as separate techniques, just one unified system of pleasing your man in the most original, creative way.

And then you can customize them by altering the firmness, application and the angle at which you use each technique.

The grip is another important element that may need to be altered to achieve the maximum desired results. You may need to go harder or softer, depending on the technique, area of application and your partner's particular preferences.

Once you have established your grip technique you can consider how it will be different depending on when in the intercourse you use it.

Do you want the handjob to be the main or even the only feature of this sexual encounter? Do you want to give him a handjob to make him come in the end? Or do you just want to introduce it as a little foreplay?

Obviously, you don't need to plan it all out exactly but at what point you will apply the handjob will determine the techniques and grip that you'll use. This is the subject of our next chapter, which will examine the flow of the handjob and how to get from the arousal state all the way to orgasm in the most efficient and satisfying manner.

For instance, a foreplay handjob can be used to build on to actual sex or a blowjob. However, if you want him to come on a certain part of your body, you knowing how to make him come with your hands will be more fun than him doing it himself.

The following tips may not apply if handjob is just a prelude or a way to end sex in this particular sexual encounter. However, if you are giving him just a handjod, the following principles will help you accomplish it.

Start off slow with a gentle up and down motion with your hand. Do this for a few minutes.
Gradually, make your motions faster as your hear his sign of approval.

If this is your first time giving a man a handjob, then remember that with practice comes professionalism and everyone starts somewhere. So do not be afraid to experiment because he will not be afraid to let you, as he acts like a lab rat waiting to be tested on. During this process, communication is key so ask him if he likes what you are doing. If he likes it, keep it up and if he doesn't don't get frustrated, just try another technique.

1. After you have gotten into a rhythm that is both stimulating to him and easy to follow through with, you will keep want to continue the same rhythm until he ejaculates.

2. If you are having trouble finding a rhythm that is relatively easy to carry out or that is pleasurable to him then try different speeds, different methods and various creative ideas such as using both hands. One hand to stimulate his sensitive areas at the head of his penis and one to stimulate an up and down motion.

3. Find his pressure gauge. Different men like different pressure and they like it in different places such as more pressure at the head or more pressure on the body. Find out how much pressure he likes and where he likes it. For each man comes different terms as to what their idea mind-blowing handjob will necessitate.

4. Another great way to find out what he likes as I have mentioned earlier in the chapter is to ask him to demonstrate. He has been giving himself handjobs since he was in his early teens, which means he is his own expert. Lay your hand atop his and ask him to show you, once you've gotten the hang of it continue the motions on your own.

5. Through-out the handjob, do not forget to use a significant amount of lubrication. In fact, you should not start a handjob unless you have a bottle of lube next to you. This will make the handjob much more pleasurable for him and the motions easier to perform.

The most important thing to watch out for when it comes to giving a handjob is his sounds and facial expressions because they will tell you everything you need to know about whether or not he is enjoying what you are doing to him. So look at his face and listen to his moans to find out if you are preparing him for the best handjob he has ever received.

## Chapter 12. The Three Main Stages.

Not to sound overly grandiose or anything, but what is the grand strategy of any handjob? This isn't rocket science but an understanding of the various stages involved in starting, maintaining and completing a handjob are essential to your proper application of the outlined techniques.

Keep in mind, that all of these stages apply only if you intend to start with a handjob and work your partner all the way through orgasm. If a handjob is a prelude, then some of these stages will not apply.

### Stage 1. The Warm Up.

At this stage your goal is to simply start the process of. It's important not to go too fast. Usually, people that are on the younger or less experienced side like to rush; but with experience comes the desire to enjoy not only the result but the whole process. So, don't rush and start it off slowly, by just rubbing or holding his balls and his penis and relying on other prelude techniques outlined in the previous chapter. As you feel the tension build, transition to the basic stroke and start utilizing some of the other techniques, gradually transitioning you to the Main Part.

### Stage 2. The Main Part.

This part is the bread and butter of your handjob. Start with the basic stroke, then move on to more Tried and True techniques, as you move on, try something more hot and stimulating like Twisting techniques. If you are aware of any of your partner's preferences when it comes to maximum arousal and stimulation, apply those here. Be sure to establish a good rhythm and gradually make the speed as well as the hardness of application more rigid. The purpose of this stage is to provide enough manual stimulation to produce maximum amount of tension. Then you can work to relieve that tension through the orgasm, which will be accomplished in the Finale. A good way to explore some more unorthodox techniques (such as those described in Backdoor Fun) would be in the middle of the main part. When you get closer to stage 3, it's time to establish a nice, constant rhythm and wait for signs that he is nearing orgasm.

Stage 3. The Finale.

Signs that your partner is nearing orgasm can vary, from him telling you to you recognizing that expression on his face. With experience, you often can feel both by how his penis pulses and other factors that he is nearing orgasm. As you feel him get closer, try to stick to the most simple and basic techniques or if you feel he is about to come because of something particular you did, just stick to doing the same thing at the same rhythm. If something feels so good he is about to come usually if you keep doing it exactly the same way, it's only a matter of time before it actually happens. As he nears orgasm, you may want to apply the basic stroke or the particular technique that you were using a little faster, adding a bit of a twisting/jerking motion to it. Talking dirty helps too, telling him how you want him to spill his hot come all over your hands. This stage is obviously the pinnacle of the whole experience. Once you feel he is about to come, maintain a nice, hard rhythm and speed it up as you feel he is about to ejaculate. Make sure you don't put pressure on him to come though; if it takes a bit longer than expected just go back to the main phase and give him more time. Pressure to perform is usually not good when it comes to sexual matters.

## Conclusion

We have learned the various simulation techniques as well as how to combine them. We've learned about creativity, inventing your own techniques and the importance to customize everything to what you and your partner feel comfortable with.

Thus, after reading this book, what would be the next step? Start with outlining techniques you'd like to try right away. Pick 1-2 that immediately struck you as cool or interesting. You don't even have to tell your partner anything, just try them with him next time you're in the bedroom.

See what works for you, what he likes and what's fun for you both. There is no precise cookie cutter system for everyone or anyone and handjobs are no exception. Succeeding at this is very much a trial and error process.

So, try a few techniques at ones, master the ones that work for both you and your partner, then work on combining them. Once you feel you've reached proficiency, add a few more techniques to spice it up. After you've mastered all the techniques the book states, move on to combinations or invent your own.

In the end, there are no particular techniques someone designed that you need to apply. You're just pleasuring your partner using your hands and this collection of techniques is a systematic way of learning to do so.

Thus, master these techniques, get plenty of practice and then set your hands free, literally. Once you have the necessary skills, creativity and spontaneity are the keys to doing any sexual performance well, and handjobs are no different.

Printed in Great
Britain
by Amazon